W9-ADY-118

Addison Mizner

FLORIDA ARCHITECTURE
of
ADDISON MIZNER

WITH A NEW INTRODUCTION BY
DONALD W. CURL

Professor of History
Florida Atlantic University

DOVER PUBLICATIONS, INC.
NEW YORK

This Dover edition, first published in 1992, is an unabridged republication of the work originally published by William Helburn, Inc., New York, in 1928. The Introduction by Donald W. Curl was written specially for the Dover edition.

Manufactured in the United States of America
Dover Publications, Inc., 31 East 2nd Street, Mineola, N.Y. 11501

Library of Congress Cataloging-in-Publication Data

Mizner, Addison, 1872–1933.
    Florida architecture of Addison Mizner / Addison Mizner, with a new introduction by Donald W. Curl.
        p.   cm.
    "An unabridged republication of the work originally published by William Helburn, Inc., New York, in 1928"—T.p. verso.
    ISBN 0-486-27327-X (pbk.)
    1. Mizner, Addison, 1872–1933—Themes, motives. 2. Eclecticism in architecture—Florida. 3. Architecture, Spanish—Florida—Influence. 4. Vacation homes—Florida. I. Title.
NA737.M59A4 1992
720′.92—dc20   92-22830
                                                                                        CIP

CONTENTS

LIST OF ILLUSTRATIONS

LIST OF ILLUSTRATIONS [*Continued*]

INTRODUCTION TO THE DOVER EDITION

Addison Mizner and Alice DeLamar

D URING THE 1920s, American publishers discovered the reading public's interest in architecture and brought out numerous volumes on individual architects' work and various architectural styles. One of the most lavish of these books, *Florida Architecture of Addison Mizner,* published in 1928, presented 184 photographs of 40 of the architect's creations in Palm Beach, Boca Raton and Jacksonville, reproduced in the rich sepia tones of the rotogravure process.

Mizner personally autographed 100 copies of a special deluxe, gold-tooled, red-Morocco-leather–bound and slipcased "Edición Imperial" of *Florida Architecture of Addison Mizner* for friends and clients. In one copy of the deluxe edition the architect wrote: "To Alice / My Lorenzo the Magnificent / Addison." Certainly Alice A. DeLamar well deserved the tribute. She had conceived of the idea for the book, aided in the photography, edited its copy, designed its pages and, after securing a publisher, subsidized its production. Calling the book a monument to Mizner—"flowers to the living instead of the dead"—DeLamar also helped sell $300 subscriptions to almost a hundred friends and clients of the architect for the deluxe edition.

When Addison Cairns Mizner (1872–1933) arrived in Palm Beach in 1918, Henry M. Flagler's Royal Poinciana and Breakers hotels dominated both the social and architectural life of the resort. Although a few pioneer resorters had built their own houses, the hotels still served as the center for society, providing the facilities for golf and tennis, and for swimming at the oceanfront Breakers' casino pool and beach. Moreover, afternoon-tea dances at the Royal Poinciana's Cocoanut Grove, multicourse dinners at both hotels and elaborate parties dedicated to special charities or marking annual observances, such as the Washington's Birthday Ball of February 22 that officially ended the season, drew hotel guests and cottagers alike.

Architecturally the Colonial Revival detailing of the wooden frame hotels, painted "Flagler yellow" with white trim, in no way reflected their semitropical setting. Theodore Blake, a draftsman for Carrère & Hastings, the New York firm that designed Flagler's St. Augustine hotels and his Palm Beach mansion, drew up the plans for the Royal Poinciana in 1893. Flagler insisted that the St. Augustine buildings should reflect that city's Spanish heritage. But although Blake had come to Carrère & Hastings from the St. Augustine concern of McDonald and McGuire (the contractors for all of Flagler's Florida buildings), there was no hint of the Spanish in his Palm Beach project. Over the years, Blake's original six-story hotel on the shores of Lake Worth grew to become a vast sprawling structure that could house 1,200 guests and seat 1,600 in its immense dining room.

The Breakers opened as the Palm Beach Inn in 1896 and proved popular with hotel guests from the first. After a 1903 fire destroyed the L-shaped four-story building, Flagler built a much larger U-shaped five-story hotel in its place. These hotels attracted America's captains of industry and its social elite. By the turn of the century, newspapers were referring to Palm Beach as "the winter Newport."

From the beginning, some vacationers preferred to own their own resort houses. Built for use only a few months of the year, the generally unpretentious shingle-style or Queen Anne cottages lined the shore of Lake Worth. Although Flagler completed Whitehall, a million-dollar white-marble mansion, in 1902 as a wedding gift for Mary Lily Kenan, his third wife, most resort cottages remained small and unostentatious until just before America entered World War I. In those years a number of winter visitors decided to build more opulent mansions and to situate them on the oceanfront. Henry Carnegie Phipps and his sister, Mrs. Frederick Guest, both had F. Burrall Hoffman, Jr., design large houses for them on the ocean. Their brother John also built a house in the same area, as did his father-in-law, Michael P. Grace. All were impressive mansions with columned porticoes and other Beaux-Arts features, but they showed no Spanish influence and would have seemed at home in any Northern resort.

By the time *Florida Architecture of Addison Mizner* was published, just a decade after Mizner came to Palm Beach, the town had been transformed both socially and architecturally. Mizner came to Palm Beach in January 1918 as the houseguest of Paris Singer, the heir to the sewing-machine fortune. Singer quickly became bored with the hotel-centered social life and decided that Palm Beach needed a private club. He had spent most of his life in Europe, and had converted houses in France and England into military hospitals as his contribution to the Allied war effort. He now commissioned Mizner to design a hospital for convalescents that could easily become a club at the war's end. When the new Everglades Club opened in 1919 the war had ended, and no veterans volunteered to recuperate in remote Palm Beach. As its owner, Singer selected a group of the most socially prominent resorters as a board of governors for the new club, and together they decided upon the applications for membership. So many applied that by the end of the season Singer announced a membership limit of 300.

From the beginning, the Everglades Club became the exclusive center for the most prominent members of resort society. The club's dramatic setting directly on the shores of Lake Worth, its romantic Spanish Revival style, with sources ranging from Alhambra courtyards to Colonial mission churches, and its innovative adaptation to the South Florida climate also made it an immediate architectural success. In typical Spanish style and as befitted an exclusive private club, the Everglades turned its back to Worth Avenue. Its major rooms opened onto secluded courtyards and the broad terrace that seemed to float over the shoreline of Lake Worth. Arcades of French doors provided both cross-ventilation (in an era before air-conditioning) and convenient access to these outdoor spaces.

Some resorters associated the Spanish style of the Everglades Club with their reason for vacationing in Palm Beach: the enjoyment of Florida's tropical winter. Others were attracted by the club's exclusive membership. This was confirmed when Eva Stotesbury, the wife of Morgan partner Edward Stotesbury and already recognized as the grande dame of Palm Beach society, commissioned Mizner to design El Mirasol, her new seaside mansion, in the Spanish style. Mizner brought to El Mirasol, his first residential commission in the resort, the innovations he had first employed in the club, and El Mirasol's plan would serve as a model for most of Mizner's large oceanfront villas. Large French doors opened onto the oceanfront terrace and the arcaded cloisters that surrounded the sheltered patios. His one-room-deep, U-shaped plan allowed for complete ventilation. He filled the courtyards with plants and grass (unlike the typical Spanish patio), allowing the vegetation to become another cooling device. He placed all the major rooms on the high ridge for the view of beach and surf; entry to the house was from the floor below. A broad staircase with elegant low risers led up to the cloister on the east side of the patio, which gave access to the dining room, living room and library. Mizner arranged the service rooms and kitchen in the northwest wing of the house; as the prevailing winter breeze came from the southeast, this prevented cooking odors from permeating the house.

By the time the 1919–20 season opened, Mizner had completed houses for the Stotesburys, Charles Munn, his brother Gurnee Munn and himself. He quickly became identified as the fashionable architect for Palm Beach society. Commissions for additional resort villas, new clubs, shops, office buildings and apartments quickly followed. All of Mizner's buildings in the resort could be labeled "Spanish," or, as the purists prefer, "Mediterranean Revival." He used barrel tiles for his roofs, though as he thought most American-made tiles had "the color of a slaughterhouse floor," he insisted on those imported from Europe or made in his own factory. Most of his buildings had rough stucco walls that provided depth and texture. He used ornamental ironwork, as well as cast-stone window frames, doorways, arches and columns, which he also manufactured. Towers and chimney pots on his roofs gave his buildings a distinctive skyline and projected height, as he found Florida "flat as a pancake." Overall, while he might borrow ideas from many sources and even different historical periods, his taste kept him from slavishly copying a design.

Mizner's style became the style of Palm Beach society. When new architects such as Marion Sims Wyeth (1889–1982), Maurice Fatio (1897–1943), Howard Major (1883–1974) and John L. Volk (1901–1984) opened Palm Beach offices, they found that clients expected them to design Mediterranean-style villas. When Mizner had arrived in 1918, Palm Beach could have passed for a New Jersey seaside resort; by 1928 it had taken on the air of a Spanish town.

Alice DeLamar first met Mizner in January 1920 through his nephew, Horace Chase, Jr. She first saw this young man on crutches, with numerous ugly red scars on his leg, leaping exuberantly in and out of the waves on the beach. Her companions immediately assumed he had suffered a serious war injury, but someone informed them that he had recently been attacked by a shark. Horace Chase and Alice DeLamar became fast friends, and before the month ended he took her to meet his uncle.

Mizner then lived at 720 South Ocean Boulevard in the first house he designed for himself, which he later sold to Harold S. Vanderbilt. DeLamar later called it an altogether charming small oceanfront house with red-tile roof and "parchment bluff" painted stucco walls. Mizner received her in a small brick-paved patio, in a jungle of banyans, cabbage palms and other wild tangled trees. A small fountain and masses of plants in assorted earthenware pots convinced Alice she was in a Mediterranean garden. She found the library–living room "a rare treat to any one who appreciated unusual taste." Spanish and Italian antique furniture, placed informally throughout the rooms, made the six-month-old house seem as if it had been comfortably inhabited for several generations. Mizner's "zoo" of chow dogs, pet raccoons, small monkeys, and parrots and macaws had complete run of the house and the patio.

DeLamar, a very sensitive woman who had a developing appreciation of art and beauty, was the product of a broken home. Moreover, her own father had died less than two years earlier. Captivated by the house and setting, and particularly by the cosmopolitan Mizner, whom she perceived as "a man of great dignity, and a very great gentleman besides being a person of great taste," she said the architect and his nephew soon "were like my own family."

Alice DeLamar's father, Captain Joseph Raphael DeLamar, was born in the Netherlands in 1843. The name was originally Spanish, an ancestor having gone to Holland as the Spanish ambassador where he married a Dutch woman and settled. Captain DeLamar came to Boston as a young man in 1859. There he became a sea captain and eventually started a marine salvage and wrecking company in Martha's Vineyard. After a near-fatal diving accident in the late 1870s he quit the sea, sold his ships and headed West. In Colorado, Nevada and Idaho he put together a mining empire.

In the early 1890s he sold these interests for approximately $20 million and moved to New York City. There he became a stock and bond investor, who was once described as "the Mystery Man of Wall Street." He also married Nellie Sands, a New Yorker who was much his junior. Alice was born on April 21, 1895, and shortly afterward the family moved to Paris. There the DeLamars divorced; Alice lived with her father, visiting her mother, now remarried, only on weekends. In 1900, when Alice turned five, she and her father returned to New York. It would be ten years before she again saw her mother.

Back in America, Captain DeLamar began construction of a very large mansion at 233 Madison Avenue on the northeast corner of 37th Street. Designed by the distinguished New York architect Charles P. H. Gilbert, the Beaux-Arts French-style *palais* was the largest on Murray Hill. At this time Captain DeLamar also began construction of Pembroke, a neoclassical "manor house of the most titanic proportions" at Glen Cove on Long Island. Though both houses had large, elegantly decorated rooms, designed for entertainment, Alice DeLamar later remembered that, with the exception of her yearly birthday party for a few

INTRODUCTION

school friends, neither she nor her father had many guests. By the time he finished the town house, Captain DeLamar had reached the age of sixty-two and, according to Alice, "had taken to his carpet slippers." She added that in this period she was "ready for rebellion" and "got along very badly with my father," who neglected her education. When she was twelve, her godfather, William Nelson Cromwell, took her education in hand and enrolled her in the Spence School. She later wrote, "It brought me the first sense of security I felt since I was five." The Spence School offered an art-history class, which kindled her lifelong interest in painting and art. In 1910 Cromwell and the school's headmistress insisted Alice be allowed to spend the summer in Paris with her mother.

After graduating from the Spence School, Alice DeLamar and a schoolmate, Evangeline Johnson, volunteered for service in Europe in the Red Cross Motor Corps, which provided ambulances to carry wounded soldiers from the battlefields of World War I. Just days after the war ended, Captain DeLamar died. Alice, his only heir, inherited the Glen Cove estate and $10 million. (Her father divided the balance of his estate of over $30 million equally among the medical schools of Harvard, Columbia and Johns Hopkins.)

Since the 1915 season, Alice DeLamar had been making regular winter visits to Palm Beach, and after her father's death she decided to make a pied-à-terre in the resort. An account in the *Palm Beach Post* said that her decision sent all the local realtors to French dictionaries in "an effort to ascertain whether it is something on a menu or a type of architecture." During the 1920 visit she and Evangeline Johnson leased a small cottage on Sunset Avenue, near the beach where she would first meet Horace Chase.

She later wrote, "With Horace and myself there was never any flirtation, or any thought of it. . . . I never failed to welcome any girl that Horace took a shine to, but he seldom specialized for long. . . . I felt myself to be a member of the family, and Horace my favorite brother; Addison my favorite uncle." Horace worked as manager of Mizner's Las Manos potteries, which the architect first established to supply Spanish-style barrel roof tiles for his many projects. DeLamar often visited the workshops and came to know Mizner's drafting rooms and the young draftsmen who worked there.

After a thorough search of the island, she bought a large ocean-to-lake tract just south of the Bolton estate. Although South Ocean Boulevard cut through the center of the land, she had 330 feet of private ocean beach and equal lake frontage. Moreover, she claimed that though "some people thought I was living way off in the jungle," she had found the "highest piece of sand dune that there was on the whole island."

She picked up drafting from watching Mizner's draftsmen work, as their activity fascinated her. Mizner drew floor plans on ruled paper and made sketches, sometimes with watercolors, of facades, and then turned the job over to the draftsmen to prepare the finished plans. "I caught onto the idea too," and with the help of the draftsmen she designed a small Venetian villa directly on the shore of Lake Worth.

A photograph in the *Palm Beach Post* in July 1922 showed the small house completely framed and roofed. The caption credited Mizner as the architect and said, "Miss DeLamar is now in Italy, making her headquarters at Florence while she selects tiles, cornices, and doors and windows for her Palm Beach place." The plans for the small villa, now in the Mizner Collection at the Historical Society of Palm Beach County, show the two-story structure with ornate Venetian Gothic windows and balconies. The ground floor included slips for a gondola and a motorboat, and service rooms, a kitchen and a garage. On the second floor, very small bedrooms surrounded a loggia that served as living and dining room.

DeLamar and the contractor had had several disagreements over design during the building of the villa; therefore, when she subsequently decided to build a small oceanfront pavilion, she drew up the plans and then found an engineer "who did not think he was an architect" to build the new house. She began the first section of what would become her large beachfront house in the mid-1920s. (Until after World War II it remained only a pavilion for bathing and picnicking by the ocean. In 1947 she completed a large wing with a master bedroom and numerous guest rooms. After she sold the lakefront half of her property, the new owners demolished the Venetian villa, and the site became the setting for an elegant Georgian-style house designed by John L. Volk.)

Both lake and ocean houses reflected DeLamar's reaction to the large mansions of her youth. She later said that for all of their large rooms and high ceilings, she found the houses gloomy and without warmth and believed that they had contributed to her unhappy childhood. Her own houses had small, almost claustrophobic rooms, though with large windows to let in the air and light.

After the death of her father Alice had moved into a Park Avenue apartment. One day a New York friend from the Red Cross invited Alice to see Carl Hamilton's collection of Early Renaissance paintings. DeLamar had dismissed her father's art as "big paintings in gold frames." However, she was "dumbfounded" and almost "transported into a dream" by Hamilton's collection, which included a Piero della Francesca, a Fra Angelico, a Fra Filippo Lippi, a Botticelli, a Mantegna and a Bellini.

It was at Hamilton's apartment that DeLamar met Bernard and Mary Berenson, who were visiting the United States. She later wrote that "we had hardly been acquainted half an hour before I suddenly felt I had found a favorite aunt and uncle and I was wholeheartedly adopted by them in return." Berenson quickly took over DeLamar's art education. During the American visit he took her to tea with Robert Lehman to see the collection that is now at the Metropolitan Museum, to the Otto Kahn mansion on upper Fifth Avenue to see his paintings, and to Boston to visit Isabella Gardner and her collection at Fenway Court. DeLamar had been to France many times, although she had never visited Italy. Before the Berensons returned home, they arranged for her to rent a villa with a superb view of Florence in Fiesole near their own villa, I Tatti, for the following summer.

During the summer, DeLamar's art-history education continued. She spent almost every morning browsing in Berenson's magnificent library, and afternoons with Mary Berenson visiting the monuments of Florence. On many warm evenings they took picnic dinners and drove to a hilltop with spectacular views of the Tuscan countryside. Once they took a four-day motor tour with Cecil Pincent, the English architect who had restored I Tatti and added the library wing to the villa.

As a wealthy young heiress, DeLamar could afford a life of connoisseurship and travel. Until the coming of World War II she spent summers in Europe, visiting the Berensons in Italy or other friends, such as the designer Hubert Givenchy, in France, where she purchased the Gerald Murphys' Paris town house. After selling her Long Island estate, she designed and built a house in Weston, Connecticut. Throughout the twenties she also maintained the Park Avenue apartment. In 1923 Mizner brought Achille Angeli, a Florentine artist who had done much of the interior painting for the restoration of the Davenzatti Palace, to paint murals for the Joshua Cosdens at Playa Riente. A 1926 newspaper article told of Angeli's painting murals for DeLamar's Park Avenue apartment and her lakefront house in Palm Beach.

Although an extremely shy and reserved person, DeLamar retained her intense interest in art and became the patron of many artists. Her aversion to publicity, however, usually led her to hide this support. She effectively became Mizner's patron when she produced the present book, but she also attempted to conceal her role in its publication.

In 1925, at the height of the Florida land boom, Mizner joined in a scheme to promote a large new subdivision in Boca Raton, twenty-five miles south of Palm Beach. Wooing investors among his former clients and society friends, he formed the Mizner Development Company and purchased over a thousand acres of land in and around the small village. In announcing plans for a grand oceanfront hotel, the company promised "the world's most architecturally beautiful playground" in the Boca Raton development.

During the next two years, Mizner poured his own fortune, the resources he could collect from investors and the down payments he received from real-estate purchasers into Boca Raton projects. These included building the small inn that ultimately became the Boca Raton Hotel and Club, the administration buildings for his sales offices and engineering staffs, a number of houses in several parts of the town, two golf courses and miles of roads and canals. The development came just at the peak of the boom. Thousands of Americans longing to get rich quick in Florida real estate made down payments on lots in Boca Raton. Unfortunately, by the summer of 1926, when many second payments came due, the blush had started to fade from the boom. Lots that had been bid higher and higher just months earlier could no longer even find buyers. Many people lacked the money for the second payment, having purchased their lots with the idea of selling at an inflated price before it fell due. Others decided to forfeit the down payment rather than invest more in what seemed a failing scheme. Then in September the Labor Day hurricane gave the coup de grace to the Florida land boom.

Although the small hotel, then called the Cloister Inn, opened in February 1927 to great acclaim, the boom had ended and Mizner had lost everything in the bust of Boca Raton. Ultimately, Clarence Geist, a Philadelphia utilities magnate and owner of a New Jersey golf club, purchased the Mizner properties in a court-ordered sale and created the Boca Raton Club. While Mizner was dedicating his efforts to the construction of Boca Raton, a number of new architects were opening offices in Palm Beach. The combination of the land bust and the new competition seriously hurt Mizner's career. Moreover, shortly after the Cloister Inn opened, Mizner was stricken with pneumonia. Though he did recover, he recuperated slowly and many of his friends worried about his future.

Alice DeLamar, one of these friends, decided to publish a book to celebrate the architect's "creative genius" and promote his failing career. Calling it a "token of appreciation by Palm Beach friends of the artistry he has accomplished here," DeLamar brought together a small group that included H. Halpine Smith, who worked in Mizner's business office, Mae Andrews, soon to become manager of Colonel Edward Bradley's Embassy Club, and Frank Geisler, the photographer. They began quietly to promote the idea of the book among Mizner's friends and former clients, selling $300 subscriptions for the deluxe edition.

Frank E. Geisler (1867–1935) was of foremost importance to the project. A nationally known and prizewinning photographer, he received highest honors at the National Exhibition of Photography in 1927 with pictures of Palm Beach's architecture and winter residents. He won a gold medal for his work at a New England "sweepstake exhibition," and had prints displayed at the Royal Society in London and at exhibits in many other cities in the United States and Europe. Geisler had a summer studio in Southampton, Long Island, and from 1917 maintained a second studio in Palm Beach during the winter season. Although best known for his portraits and landscapes, his earlier photographs of Mizner's Palm Beach buildings had appeared in respected journals such as *Architectural Forum* and *Arts and Decoration*. He agreed to contribute these earlier prints, such as his 1919 photographs of the Everglades Club and of Mizner's own first small house, to the project and to photograph other buildings especially for the new volume.

DeLamar, who would involve herself in every aspect of the book's production, believed that any photograph of a building facade taken from ground level contained too much distortion. She therefore built a platform on the bed of an old Ford truck she owned and drove Geisler around to the various houses. "All the outdoor shots were taken from the platform on top of my old truck, and old man Gizler [*sic*] climbed up a ladder and thought it was a good idea." Altogether, he produced 185 illustrations for the book. His portrait of Mizner, which DeLamar considered the best ever taken of the architect, served as the book's frontispiece.

Paris Singer also joined the project. Over the years he and Mizner had remained friends. Mizner had designed an addition to the Everglades Club in

INTRODUCTION

1919 that almost doubled its size and included a large new apartment for Singer. Although Singer sometimes mentioned commissioning a Mizner house, he said, "Each house Addison builds is more beautiful than the one before, so I want to eventually live in the last house Addison will build, and that will be his best one of all." This respect for Mizner's talent comes through in Singer's short foreword, where, likening Mizner to a medieval architect and master of all crafts, he said his work "will live in the history of American Architecture when we are gone and forgotten."

Ida M. Tarbell, who had gained fame for her muckraking articles on the Standard Oil Trust, contributed an introduction, the bulk of which grew from a long interview with Mizner in his fifth-floor study, with the red-tiled roofs of the town of Palm Beach visible from every window. Mizner told her the anecdotes that he later used in his own autobiography: stories of his pioneering California family, his youth spent in Central America, his adventures in Alaska and in the South Seas, and his training in Guatemala, Spain and California to become an architect—all the tales that Mizner used to amuse Palm Beach resorters. As Singer said in his foreword, Mizner was "the most delightful and entertaining of men." As the resort's leading society architect, Mizner attended all the major social functions and most of the fashionable private parties. As a raconteur and talented gossip, hostesses found him the perfect "extra man," and he needed the extensive social life to meet the prospective clients who would fuel his professional life. Nonetheless, Mizner remained a very private person, and Tarbell's introduction tells us little about that private man.

Mizner identified the various commissions for DeLamar, and she chose the photographs and wrote the captions. On February 7, 1928, Mizner received the Singer and Tarbell texts for approval and immediately wrote to DeLamar in New York that "it is perfectly O.K., and as far as that goes, everything you do is O.K."

William Helburn, Inc., published the completed work near the end of March 1928. The clothbound edition cost twenty dollars. The reviewers, both in the popular press and in professional journals, consistently praised the work. One called the book as monumental as Mizner's architecture, another termed it "remarkable," while still another called it a revelation that "should certainly be in the library of every lover of Florida—and every lover of Beauty." One insightful reviewer noted that "Mizner has not transplanted Spanish forms in Florida—rather has he taken the essence of Spanish work and developed from it a new architecture, one that really fits the breeze-swept, sun-swept, gay, leisurely Southland." The critic for *Architectural Forum* found the volume "one of the most handsomely designed and printed contributions to the architect's library to appear in many a day. The paper is fine, and the page design and typing of a quality seldom met with in the field of architectural publication."

Alice DeLamar, obviously extremely proud of her accomplishment, retained copies of all of the reviews. Perhaps a note from Mizner that arrived during the summer of 1928 meant even more to her:

Carmel Valley, 17 Miles from
Monterey California

My dearest Alice

    I have been so ill since *The* Book took shape that I have never made it quite clear how much I appreciated the greatest compliment ever payed a living architect. I should be very conceited about it; but it has had just the opposite effect for now I will have to do something to justify myself. The house I am doing at Santa Barbara [Casa Bienvenita, for Alfred E. Dieterich; actually in Montecito] is I think my very best. I will send you pictures of it next spring. Also I am doing one in Philadelphia [La Ronda, for Percival E. Foerderer; on Mount Pleasant Road in Bryn Mawr] which I am interested in and I hope it isn't going to shame you.

    I have bought a ranch up the Carmel Valley and have fixed up a shack so that I can be out here each summer. I feel a great deal better. Ysabel [his niece Ysabel Chase, for whom he designed a house in Pebble Beach] is fine and is helping me with the garden.

Always devotedly
Addison

    Mizner died on February 5, 1933, just five years after the publication of *Florida Architecture of Addison Mizner*. In his later years he designed only a few additional Florida projects. In 1928 he completed the Spanish Colonial–style residence for Jerome D. Gedney in Manalapan, a brokerage office for John F. Harris on Collins Avenue in Miami Beach, and a nurses' residence for Harris at Good Samaritan Hospital in West Palm Beach. Mizner also completed The Cloisters (a small hotel) and a house, for Alfred Jones, Sr., both on Sea Island, Georgia, and the two houses that he mentions in his note. In 1929 Mizner and Lester Geisler designed the Embassy Club for Colonel Edward R. Bradley on Royal Palm Way in Palm Beach, which is today the gallery of the Society of the Four Arts. That same year Mizner completed the Memorial Fountain and Plaza north of the Town Hall in Palm Beach, and three shops on South County Road at Seaview Avenue, and remodeled the original house of Nate Spingold on Wells Road. In 1930 his only completed project was a brokerage office for E. F. Hutton on South County Road at the entrance to Phipps Plaza. In 1931 he designed his last large Florida villa, Casa Coe da Sol, on Park Street North in St. Petersburg, for William J. Williams. He also designed an apartment for the publisher Oscar G. Davies in the Palm Beach Daily News Building on South County Road. Finally, in 1932 he completed a small residence for K. D. Alexander on Brazilian Avenue in Palm Beach, and the Everglades Theater (a small movie house) for Hugo Gold in Belle Glade.

    With the stock-market collapse in 1929 and the coming of the Great Depression, fewer Palm Beach clients wished to invest in the large, ostentatious mansions of the early twenties. Major Alley, a small apartment complex designed in the Bermuda style by Howard Major, had introduced a more modest architecture to the resort as early as 1925. Now Palm Beachers, wishing to make "less show of their money," asked for smaller houses in traditional Georgian and British Colonial styles.

INTRODUCTION

In many ways, *Florida Architecture of Addison Mizner* served as an epitaph for the man, his style and the era. The beautifully designed book with its antique-looking Baskerville type and the sepia rotogravure-reproduced photographs seemed to speak of an earlier, more gracious period. While Alice DeLamar's work made Mizner the best-known Florida architect of the 1920s and presented his work to a very large audience of professional architects and laymen, it also seemed to seal it in time. As Palm Beachers looked to less lavish and costly traditional architecture, and much of the rest of the Western world looked to the modernists and their cleaner and purer lines, Mizner's creations as they appeared in *Florida Architecture of Addison Mizner* looked old-fashioned and from a bygone era.

In fact, the next half-century was extremely unkind to Mizner and his work. Critics attacked his buildings as stage sets and copies of postcards or pictures from architectural magazines and books. In 1953 Alva Johnston, a writer for *The New Yorker,* published a dual biography of Addison and his brother Wilson. Johnston later admitted that in *The Legendary Mizners* he deliberately fictionalized Addison's life to make it more colorful. While Johnston was researching the book, Alice DeLamar had typed a sixty-page letter to him that painted a picture of the architect remarkably different from the one Johnston eventually published. For DeLamar, Mizner was a man of exquisite taste, broad and extensive learning and great sensitivity to his surroundings and to other people. She told Johnston of Mizner's abilities as an architect, craftsman and painter and provided an insightful view of his life as a pillar of the Palm Beach community. Moreover, she named dozens of people who had known Mizner for Johnston to interview.

Unfortunately, Johnston ignored all of her efforts. DeLamar later said, "The name of Alva Johnston is really anathema to me, and I think he wrote a dreadful book. Mr. Mizner was like a very favorite uncle to me, he was a very great gentleman and all his innumerable friends really did love him. . . . You would not get that impression from [Johnston] who was only interested in collecting bar room type anecdotes. . . . He never bothered to look up [any of the people I suggested]." Nonetheless, Johnston produced a very popular book, and in the minds of his readers Mizner became the architect of little background or training who drew plans in the sand at the beach, forgot to include stairways, baths and kitchens in his houses, said "buildings first, plans later" and hid in closets to escape his clients.

The 1950s and 1960s also saw the destruction of many of Mizner's finest houses. In the "barefoot era," the typically large Mizner house seemed too formal. Palm Beachers now spent most of the year in town. They found the large Mizner mansions too difficult to air-condition and very expensive to maintain. Meanwhile, the age-old problem of Palm Beach, finding sufficient staff, became particularly acute during the period after World War II. Of the twenty-eight residences pictured in *Florida Architecture of Addison Mizner,* seven have been destroyed. At least another seven have been significantly altered. Thus, only half of that architectural heritage remains.

El Mirasol, his first great Palm Beach mansion, was also the first to meet the wrecking ball. After Edward Stotesbury's death in May 1938, his wife Eva discovered that his once-immense fortune had dwindled to only a few million dollars and that her income was inadequate to support her three mansions in Philadelphia, Bar Harbor and Palm Beach. Within the next few years she sold her Northern estates and began to subdivide the forty-two acres of El Mirasol. When she died in 1946 only twelve oceanfront acres surrounding the house remained. The Pittsburgh Company, one of the many corporations owned by the Phipps family, purchased El Mirasol. The house was razed in the mid-1950s, and in 1964 Robert Gottfried developed El Mirasol Estates, a subdivision of fourteen lots.

Shortly after Joshua Cosden moved into Playa Riente, Mizner's most magnificent oceanfront villa, he suffered financial difficulties and placed it on the market. In April 1926 Mrs. Horace Dodge, widow of the automaker, paid $2.8 million for the estate. Hugh Dillman, a former actor who was now manager of the Society of the Arts and a real-estate agent, represented Mrs. Dodge in the sale. Three weeks later in Detroit, Mrs. Dodge married Dillman in a private ceremony. After returning from their honeymoon, the Dillmans asked Mizner to add a great 120-foot-square "Gothic-Moorish" cloister to the house. He chose the cloister of the Monastery of San Juan de los Reyes at Toledo as his model, though he designed a one-story version of the original. Rose-tinted cast-stone rib vaulting, springing from elaborately molded scroll brackets, supported the twenty-foot-high ceilings. Mizner Industries' cast-stone pointed arches, filled with Moresque tracery, surrounded the interior patio. A large "Gothic-finished" room in one corner of the cloister served as Dillman's study.

At the time of the Dillmans' marriage, newspaper reporters pointed out the difference in their ages, and many in Palm Beach predicted an early divorce. When they ended their marriage twenty-one years later (certainly by Palm Beach standards a fairly long time), Mrs. Dillman resumed the Dodge name. She also found Playa Riente far too large for the few months a year she spent in Palm Beach. When she tried to sell it, she found no market for estates of that size. In 1952, as the cost of upkeep and taxes continued to rise, Mrs. Dodge applied for a zoning change to allow Playa Riente to be used as a club or school. When the town council refused she began a long court battle, which ended five years later with the town's zoning decision upheld.

Angered by her court defeat, Mrs. Dodge, now nearly ninety years old, decided to hold an auction of the contents, raze the mansion and sell the land. Though many local groups tried to save the house, they made little headway in finding the $1.2 million she demanded. In early March 1957 Mrs. Dodge opened the house for tours, the benefits of which were to go to the Good Samaritan Hospital. The sale of the contents came three days later, and by Christmas Playa Riente was only a memory.

Casa Bendita, the John S. Phipps mansion, stood for less than forty years. During its construction in 1922, its size prompted one newspaper article to call it "Phipps' Castle." Located just north of El Mirasol and Heamaw, the house of

John's brother Henry Carnegie Phipps, Casa Bendita's major rooms faced the ocean from high on the beach ridge. On the west the house surrounded a large courtyard on three sides. Its southern wing contained guest rooms on the second floor and a colonnaded swimming pool underneath. Casa Bendita remained Phipps's Palm Beach residence until his death in 1958. Although his son Michael retained ownership of the land on the west side of County Road, in December 1960 he sold the house and the oceanfront part of the property to a Cleveland real-estate developer who planned an "exclusive residential park" on the 376-foot ocean frontage. In February 1961 the Big Chief Wrecking Company began its work, and by the end of the month the last of the beautiful old mansion had been hauled away to the dump.

Mizner designed Casa Florencia, one of his most beautiful houses, for the Preston Pope Satterwhites. He had known Florence Satterwhite in New York, and she had been a member of the party during his first visit to Palm Beach in 1908. The Satterwhites were demanding clients, insisting on an appropriate background for their growing art collection. The house pleased them so much that they decided upon what one writer called "a Renaissance gesture." They commissioned Percival Dietsch, a sculptor who had done the bas-reliefs over several doors at Playa Riente, to execute a bas-relief portrait of the architect for the keystone over the stairway window. When Mrs. Satterwhite died in May 1927, only four years after commissioning the house, Dr. Satterwhite placed Casa Florencia on the market. John North Willys, the Toledo automaker, purchased the house in 1929. His daughter later inherited the property; in 1952 she tore down Casa Florencia because "it was too big," and built a ranch-style house on the site. The remains of the Satterwhite villa, and presumably the bas-relief of Mizner, are buried under a large mound in the front yard of the new house.

Mizner's large 1923 house for Joseph Speidel followed his usual oceanfront plan, with the main entrance on the basement level, a grand staircase leading up to the living and dining rooms and a loggia overlooking the beach. Since the lot stretched from ocean to lake, the 36-by-24-foot living room had views of both. The house was demolished early in the 1960s, and in 1967 John L. Volk designed a modern house with Chinese detailing and a pagoda-style roof for the lot.

Legend claims that when Mizner asked William Wood, "the woolen king," if he had any preferences for the design of his new house, he replied that he liked towers. By the time of publication of *Florida Architecture of Addison Mizner*, Wood had committed suicide and Stephen A. Lynch of Atlanta had purchased The Towers. Later it stood vacant for several years until Atwater Kent, the radio manufacturer, bought it in 1936. Before the Kents moved in, John L. Volk modernized the house, removing most of the Spanish interior wood paneling and ceilings and the tilework. At the end of World War II Kent moved to California, and Robert Young, chairman of the New York Central Railroad, and his wife Anita, a sister of the artist Georgia O'Keeffe, acquired The Towers. The extremely social Youngs entertained the Duke and Duchess of Windsor every year. In January 1958 Robert Young committed suicide in The Towers, giving it its reputation as Mizner's most tragic house. In the summer of 1964, Mrs. Young had the mansion razed after an elegant "last fling" dinner and card party, with the Duke and Duchess among the guests.

The most recently demolished Mizner-designed mansion in Palm Beach was the George Luke Mesker house, La Fontana, located on South Ocean Boulevard at Royal Palm Way. Mesker, an Evansville, Indiana, industrialist, built the sixteenth-century Italian Renaissance–style house in 1923. In the early 1930s Maurice Fatio remodeled the house, completely changing its character. In association with the decorator Charles Duveen of London, Fatio added a third-story tower bedroom for Mesker, numerous bay windows with small panes of stained glass and a seventeenth-century pub brought over complete—from pegged floor to fireplace—from England.

The Wallaford Ransom Leaches of Atlanta acquired the now Tudor-style house in 1948 after Mrs. Mesker's death. In 1966 the town allowed the construction of an apartment building just to the south of La Fontana on Ocean Boulevard. As the apartments overlooked the Leaches' walled patios, the Leaches immediately requested that the town rezone their property as well to permit apartment construction. When refused, they sued, and in 1968 the court ordered rezoning. The Leaches then sold the house to a syndicate headed by the former ambassador Matthew McCloskey, which tore it down and built a large six-story condominium on the site.

Many Palm Beach preservationists believed that within a few short years all the large gracious mansions of the twenties would be only memories. Developers also razed many of the large houses of other architects and physically divided many mansions to create several houses. This happened to Mizner's mansions for John Magee at 1560 South Ocean Boulevard and Barclay Harding Warburton at 480 Worth Avenue. In 1974 Barbara Hoffstot published *Landmark Architecture of Palm Beach*. Both a dedicated preservationist and a lifelong resident of the resort, Hoffstot appealed to Palm Beachers to save their town and lobbied the town council to pass a landmarks ordinance. A few years later, Christina Orr curated a show of Mizner drawings and photographs and the products of his industries, which helped to dispel some of the Mizner myths and convince people to take his architecture more seriously.

In this more favorable atmosphere for preservation, the town council denied permission for a developer to raze the William Gray Warden house, one of the last great Mizner mansions remaining in the town. The developer sued, and the controversy won more converts for preservation. At the last minute, Robert Eigelberger bought and restored the mansion and secured permission to convert it into six condominium apartments. Moreover, the controversy over the Warden house also helped convince the town council to pass the landmarks-preservation ordinance and create the Landmarks Commission.

During this time, Alice DeLamar continued to defend Mizner's reputation and to protect his work. She wrote long, detailed letters to Christina Orr about the architect's life and lent many pieces for the Mizner exhibit. When, in March

INTRODUCTION

1983, the new Landmarks Commission attempted to designate an historic district that included Worth Avenue, the president of the Everglades Club, which owned twenty-three shops and boutiques on the avenue, wrote to members asking them to protest the action: "It isn't the facades of the buildings which attract people but what is behind them . . . the merchandise and the manner in which it is displayed. Here they find a unique concentration of art, jewelry, and high fashion clothing and accessories not duplicated anywhere else." DeLamar, whose club membership dated back to 1926, immediately replied that since most of the stores on the street were outlets of large chains, the merchandise could be found across the country. The architecture gave Worth Avenue its importance and, according to DeLamar, needed the protection of the Landmarks Commission. As to merchants' knowing best how to present their goods, DeLamar said that, given the "quite atrocious" taste of most storekeepers, if the town failed to act the street could soon look like "any Miami shopping street. . . . I am not in favor of encouraging change—what we have here is unique; let us preserve [Worth Avenue] as best we can that it may be admired by many future generations."

Alice DeLamar had kept a number of copies of *Florida Architecture of Addison Mizner*. These she often presented anonymously as gifts to libraries of historical societies and architectural schools. She also continued to sell copies of the book. A 1968 newsletter of the Historical Society of Palm Beach County mentioned that the Colony Book Shop had two copies of the "magnificently illustrated volume." Sometime in the early 1980s she sold the remaining unbound pages to a Floridiana bookseller, who trimmed the pages and, using a library binding, produced a less elegant though more manageable book.

DeLamar, who had grown even more reclusive and shy in her later years, was horrified to discover herself in the national news in 1979, when a retired businessman discovered a long-lost certificate of stock in the Texas Pacific Land Trust. The certificate had belonged to Captain DeLamar, who may have lost it through the failure of a brokerage house in 1907. Transfers, mergers and stock splits had since turned the original 100 shares into 20,000 shares worth $1.72 million and 53,456 shares of Texaco stock worth $1.5 million, and about $800,000 in dividends had been deposited in a custody account over the years. The wire story said that Alice DeLamar "has a flock of servants and no living relatives," and concluded, "The news that she may be $2 million richer seems to have had about as much impact as finding a $5 bill on the sidewalk." Unfortunately, DeLamar died before the courts settled the ownership of the certificate.

Although DeLamar still had "a flock of servants," she needed the money. In the spring of 1983 she received an offer of $2.5 million for her Palm Beach house, with the proviso that she could retain residence for life. A second requirement called for the removal of the historic designation on the property so that the new owner could demolish the house after DeLamar's death. The attorney who represented DeLamar before the Landmarks Commission said she needed the money "to continue her current life style." Moreover, DeLamar claimed the house had little historical significance and, since she had designed it herself, little architectural merit. The Landmarks Commission agreed, one member saying it was "too personal and small" for landmark status.

Alice DeLamar died in August 1983, only a few months after the commission voted to rescind the designation. In May 1984 the new owner demolished the DeLamar house, planning to build a large new mansion on the 3.7 secluded oceanfront acres. These plans fell through, but in the autumn of 1987 Robert Gottfried began construction of a 27,000-square-foot Mediterranean-style villa on the property. It sold in early 1992 for $9 million, the highest price ever paid for a new house in Florida.

Alice DeLamar would have been disheartened to learn that the demolition of her house would be followed by the leveling of a series of historic houses. In August 1985 the Douglas–Williams–Wrightsman house at 513 North County Road, designed originally by H. Hastings Mundy and added to by Marion Sims Wyeth and Maurice Fatio, met the fate of The Towers, its former neighbor to the north. The next year another Fatio-designed oceanfront house, at 601 North County Road, was also demolished. Commissioned by Edward V. Quinn in 1937, it was last owned by Colonel Michael Paul. Just a year before its demolition, a newspaper article suggested Buckingham Palace might choose the house as the residence for the Prince and Princess of Wales on their Palm Beach visit. In 1987 a Chicago investment broker asked the town's permission to demolish The Plantation, a house on Wells Road at the lakefront designed by John L. Volk in 1932 and one of the earliest British Colonial–style houses in Palm Beach. In this same period, Mizner's own third house at 1800 South Ocean Boulevard, which he later sold to Edward Small Moore, was so seriously altered that the town removed it from the list of designated properties. Only a national recession slowed this trend.

As houses are destroyed, modernized, added to and divided, the Mediterranean Revival character of Palm Beach's architecture grows fainter with each passing year. Although the Landmarks Commission and the Preservation Foundation of Palm Beach attempt to preserve some of the earlier heritage, it is an endless battle. One can only hope that *Florida Architecture of Addison Mizner*, Alice DeLamar's loving tribute to the architect, will never become just a memorial to that earlier era.

DONALD W. CURL
FLORIDA ATLANTIC UNIVERSITY
BOCA RATON

CHECKLIST OF MIZNER BUILDINGS,
IN ORDER SHOWN IN PHOTOGRAPHS

(Except as noted, buildings are still standing, essentially in their original state.)

Residence of Addison Mizner, Via Mizner, 341 Worth Avenue, Palm Beach. 1924. (Plates 1-9)

Via Mizner, 341 Worth Avenue, Palm Beach. Many alterations over the years. 1923-24. (Pl. 10-12)

Via Parigi, 353 Worth Avenue, Palm Beach. 1925. (Pl. 13, 14)

Worth Avenue, arcade of shops [Villa Mizner and the Mizner Studio and Shops], 341 Worth Avenue, Palm Beach. 1923-24. (Pl. 15)

Everglades Club, 356 Worth Avenue, Palm Beach. 1919+. Alterations and additions by Marion Sims Wyeth and John L. Volk. (Pl. 16-32)

Singer Building, 441 Royal Palm Way, Palm Beach. 1925. Alterations by John L. Volk, 1947. (Pl. 33)

The Plaza Shops, 240-246 South County Road at Phipps Plaza, Palm Beach. 1924. (Pl. 34, 35)

The Gulfstream Golf Club, 2401 North Ocean Boulevard, Gulf Stream. 1923. (Pl. 36-39)

The Cloister [Inn] at Boca Raton, 501 East Camino Real, Boca Raton. 1925. Additions and alterations by Schultze & Weaver, Marion Sims Wyeth, Maurice Fatio and others. (Pl. 40-55)

Administration Building at Boca Raton, Camino Real and Dixie Highway, Boca Raton. 1925. (Pl. 56-58)

Riverside Baptist Church, Park and King Streets, Jacksonville. Bruce Kitchell, associate architect. 1926. (Pl. 59-61)

El Sarimento, residence of A. J. Drexel Biddle, Jr., 150 South Ocean Boulevard, Palm Beach. 1923. Additions and alterations by Joseph Urban and Maurice Fatio. (Pl. 62-64)

*Residence of Arthur B. Claflin, 800 South County Road, Palm Beach. 1923. (Pl. 65-72)

Playa Riente, residence of Mrs. Hugh Dillman [Mrs. Horace Dodge] (formerly of Joshua S. Cosden), 947 North Ocean Boulevard, Palm Beach. 1923. Demolished in 1957. (Pl. 73-87)

Casa De Leoni, residence of Robert Glendinning (formerly of Leonard Thomas), 450 Worth Avenue, Palm Beach. 1921. (Pl. 88-90)

Residence of John F. Harris, 4 El Bravo Way, Palm Beach. Original residence designed by Marion Sims Wyeth, 1920. Mizner added the tower and remodeled the original house, 1928. (Pl. 91-93)

Residence of Harry Haskins (formerly of Hon. C[harles] J. W[i]nn), 121 El Bravo Way, Palm Beach. 1921. Additions by Marion Sims Wyeth. (Pl. 94)

*La Bellucia, residence of Dr. Willey Lyon Kingsley, 1200 South Ocean Boulevard, Palm Beach. 1920. (Pl. 95–97)

The Towers, residence of Stephen A. Lynch (formerly of William M. Wood), 548 North County Road, Palm Beach. 1923. Demolished in 1964. (Pl. 98)

Residence of H. P. McGinley (formerly of Daniel H. Carstairs), 280 North Ocean Boulevard, Palm Beach. 1923. Additions by Maurice Fatio. (Pl. 99–102)

Residence of George Luke Mesker [La Fontana], Royal Palm Way and South Ocean Boulevard, Palm Beach. 1923. Alterations by Maurice Fatio. Demolished in 1968. (Pl. 103–105)

Residence of Wilson Mizner, 237 Worth Avenue, Palm Beach. 1924. A store building now shields the house from the street. (Pl. 106)

Sin Cuidado, residence of Edward S. Moore (Mizner's own third residence), 1800 South Ocean Boulevard, Palm Beach. 1922. Alterations by Maurice Fatio; later remodeled so that none of the original historic facade remains. (Pl. 107–113)

Collado Hueco, residence of Paul Moore, 1820 South Ocean Boulevard, Palm Beach. 1924. (Pl. 114–17)

*Louwana, residence of Gurnee Munn, 473 North County Road, Palm Beach. 1919, 1923. (Pl. 118, 119)

*Amado, residence of Charles Munn, 455 North County Road, Palm Beach. 1919. (Pl. 120, 121)

Casa Bendita, residence of John S. Phipps, 434 North County Road, Palm Beach. 1921. Demolished in 1961. (Pl. 122–25)

Residence of George S. Rasmussen [Casa Nana], 780 South Ocean Boulevard, Palm Beach. 1926. Addition by Jeffrey A. Smith, 1991. (Pl. 126, 127)

Lagomar, residence of Henry Rea (formerly of John Magee), 1560 South Ocean Boulevard, Palm Beach. 1924. House divided into several parts and estate subdivided. (Pl. 128–32)

Villa Tranquilla, residence of De Grimm Renfro, 100 El Brillo Way, Palm Beach. 1923. Additions by Marion Sims Wyeth. (Pl. 133, 134)

Casa Florencia, residence of Dr. Preston Pope Satterwhite, 910 South Ocean Boulevard, Palm Beach. 1923. Demolished in 1952. (Pl. 135–44)

Villa Flora, residence of Edward Shearson, 110 Dunbar Avenue (at North Ocean Boulevard), Palm Beach. 1923. (Pl. 145–47)

Concha Marina, residence of George Sloan[e] (Mizner's own second house), 102 Jungle Road (at South Ocean Boulevard), Palm Beach. 1921. Additions and alterations by Marion Sims Wyeth, Maurice Fatio, John L. Volk and others. (Pl. 148, 149)

Residence of Joseph Speidel [Casa Joseto], 942 South Ocean Boulevard, Palm Beach. 1923. Demolished in late 1950s or early 1960s. (Pl. 150, 151)

El Mirasol, residence of Edward T. Stotesbury, 348 North County Road, Palm Beach. 1919. Demolished in early 1950s. (Pl. 152–64)

INTRODUCTION

El Salano, residence of Harold Vanderbilt (Mizner's own first house), 720 South Ocean Boulevard, Palm Beach. 1919, 1920. Additions by Maurice Fatio. (Pl. 165–68)

La Guerida, residence of Rodman Wanamaker (today better known as the Kennedy House), 1113 North Ocean Boulevard, Palm Beach. 1923. Additions by Maurice Fatio. (Pl. 169–70)

Casa Maria Marrone, residence of Barclay Warburton, 480 Worth Avenue, Palm Beach. 1922. Additions by Howard Major, Lester Geisler and Marion Sims Wyeth; now divided into several houses. (Pl. 171–74)

Residence of William Gray Warden, 112 Seminole Avenue (at North Ocean Boulevard), Palm Beach. 1922. Restored and converted into six condominium units in 1983. (Pl. 175–84)

---

*No access, or cannot be seen from street.

FOREWORD

I T IS NOW ten years since Addison Mizner and I came to Palm Beach. The beauty of the country, the delight of the climate so captivated us from the start that we stayed on; but we were both too active-minded to lie around in the sun doing nothing. The Great War was still on and I decided to build a hospital for wounded officers; Addison was to be the architect.

He took hold of the work with astonishing energy and enthusiasm but it was a tough task. He had great difficulty in finding workmen in Florida who understood his requirements, but that never daunted him. When he could find no one to carry out his orders, he set to with his own hands and made the thing he wanted. He could do this for he is, like the architects of the Middle Ages, a master of all the crafts that serve his profession. He paints, carves wood, and works in metals, knows all about the making of glazed pottery and his wrought iron is second to none in Old Spain.

Before our hospital was finished the Peace came along and we decided to turn our building into a Club—the Everglades.

The place took the town by storm, so remarkable was the sense of proportion, composition and color shown in the buildings, the gardens and patios. On the strength of what Mizner was doing in the Everglades Club, Mr. and Mrs. E. T. Stotesbury asked him to design a villa for them, and this was followed rapidly by orders from other leading visitors.

Mizner's buildings in Palm Beach now can be counted by the dozens, yet all are dissimilar and distinctive of his genius. They are so subtly adapted to this State and its warm climate that, although inspired by the art of Spain and Italy, they are an order of Architecture of his own which will live in the history of American Architecture when we are gone and forgotten.

My friend Mizner, however, is more than a great architect, he is the most delightful and entertaining of men. From his tall, imposing presence one would never think that his health is far from robust. He is always cheerful and hearty and his mastery of Tavern English is a joy to everybody within hearing. He gives the impression that his life is all laughter and fun, yet I know of few men who have produced as much original and splendid work in ten short years.

Paris Singer

ADDISON MIZNER

APPRECIATION OF A LAYMAN

THE MONTH was February — the year 1926, and I was motoring from Miami to Palm Beach, Florida. So far as outward signs went the boom was still at its height. The one feature that had admittedly disappeared was the rascally "binder boy," and as he was never a Floridian but an uninvited intruder from the crooked places of certain great Northern cities, there was glee and satisfaction at his retirement, particularly as he had gone because they had caught him, in clever Miami, in the same kind of trap, in which he for some months had been catching them. The binder boy was gone, but everything else was running at top speed—excavators, sand-suckers, hopes, spell binders, free lunches, openfaced offices, whippets, auto busses, presses. On every side of the Dixie Highway by which I was traveling north, there was frenzied sub-dividing, lot staking, tearing down of old towns, laying out of new. Never had I seen so continuous a stretch of benevolent devastation.

And it was harder on me because at every mile of the way I was called upon to admire—not what was before my eyes, but the vision before the eyes of my guides. All Florida at that moment saw visions—completed things, apparently the day when every acre of its soil had been transformed into town lots, with white villas set in palms, backed by orange and banana groves and always with a water front, natural or artificial. They might achieve it. I had seen glittering cities rising where a year before there was only a snake-infested mangrove swamp. Anything was possible in Florida, yet my eyes were the eyes of the uninspired and whatever my tongue said, in the depths of my heart I pronounced it hideous.

It was, I told myself bitterly, as hateful as the roads of devastated France over which I had motored seven years ago that very month—with a difference.

There it had been the sinister and despairing devastation left by war, here it was the joyful and confident devastation of development—a very great difference indeed!

WHEN WE suddenly left the congested and tormented highway, driving into an avenue two hundred or so feet wide, without a ditch or a sand-sucker or a pile of concrete blocks in sight—a broad, uncrowded way, the land on either side unscarred, the lovely and mysterious half jungle still green and rampant.

Boca Raton—I had been lured there by the name, its smell of mystery and pirates, but I expected to find the usual upheaval of development. Instead I found Florida as I once had dreamed it, and as it was before the hand of the speculator and the builder had been laid so heavily on its enchantment. Still, Boca Raton was a development, and I was going to lunch at the hotel with which a development always begins in Florida. It would probably be like all the rest. But no. We came unobstructedly to its entrance. There was no more sign of destructive progress here than there had been along the avenue. There was order, a certain completeness; and I gasped as I gave a swift glance at the building to which I had come—it was so beautiful, so cool and quiet and confidently beautiful.

"Somebody built that who knew what he was about," flashed into my mind as I saw "The Cloister," for that was what they called this first hotel in Boca Raton. I was quite right. And the impression deepened the next hour or two as I went over the place with the man who had made it—Addison Mizner.

THE CLOISTER was simple to severity in its whole yet rich in delights. Red tiled roofs rambled up and down, spreading comfortably in every direction as in old world buildings which have been added to, time and again. There was a square tower for height; there was a great court and arcades with round arches and capitals alive with animals and grotesque figures; there were innumerable details that held the eye not alone for their beauty but for their knowledge of the type which had inspired the place; and every here and there was introduced some rare finding brought from Spain itself,— like the wooden beams and carved brackets worked into the cloister, pieces which had come from the old University of Seville, a good part of which Mizner seems to have freighted over to this country.

The building rose from the shores of a little lake, its lounge hanging over the water. It was easy not only to "see things" but to believe them, looking across the lake from this lounge and listening to Addison Mizner talk of his plans for Boca Raton. For the first time since I had come to Florida I had an inner sense of what vision meant. I had not believed it before, I did now. I saw with special clearness a cathedral "just over there"— a cathedral which the architect had been dreaming of for " Mamma Mizner," as he calls his mother. She must have been as lovely and gracious as she was an indomitable great lady, this "Mamma Mizner," of whom a word later.

IN THE following days I saw more of Addison Mizner's handiwork—work that had been done in Palm Beach in the eight previous years—houses great and small, a famous club, a street, his own house. There was no choosing from the things that I saw, although they were so vastly different in scale and purpose, and this seemed to me a final convincing proof of his knowing what he was about.

Not only that. He was not in the least afraid of the Spanish type in which he worked. It seemed to me that it was so much a part of him that he could play with it, adapt it joyously and surely to any location, any purse; and, what was quite as important,—though architects do not always think it—he could help the people for whom he had built, to live in the things he made for them.

I got an impression as I went about that after he had built, decorated and furnished their houses, he was keeping in loving touch with the people for whom he had made all these things, helping them to enjoy them as he himself, their creator, enjoyed them.

THERE WAS an extraordinary practical sense in his houses—places for things—all sorts of things. No woman was left without ample shelves for her slippers and shoes, even if they ran into the hundred or more pairs—and every house was planned with the kitchen on the northeast corner. The prevailing wind is southwest. Smells blow into the house if you put your kitchen where that wind can catch them. "Required considerable study," Mizner admitted!

One of his passions in building is windows—never too many—and every room must have a cross draft. I never found one that did not. I remember a little house—that is, they called it little—one of the first that he had built, I believe. It stood on the sandy ridge that the ocean throws up just back of the beach. Behind the elevation lie bodies of water, canals and lagoons; and Mizner had run a house—a long, low house—along that ridge, every window with a water view, almost every one with two—one of the ocean, the other of the quiet pools. And such were the windows, so many and so big, that one had the feeling that inside the house he was as much in the marvelous Florida air as if on the beach or in the garden without.

HE SEEMED to me to have a veritable passion for utilizing all of the marvelous natural beauties of the place, and that was the more precious to me because I had often been heavy-hearted in Florida over what appeared an amazing indifference to the fascinations of the country, an inability to catch and emphasize her real charms, to make a typical Floridian thing. That the succession of builders who have in the past undertaken developments in Florida should have thought architecturally in terms of Saratoga frame hotels, Middle West Queen Anne cottages or bleak New England farm houses, is the more puzzling when they had before their eyes so beautiful an example of what really belongs there, of what the place cries for as the simple adaptation of the Spanish that one finds at Saint Augustine. It is more puzzling still when you realize that they have, one may say, in their front yard particularly on the East shore, "the makin's" for a Spanish house—coquina, ojus, coral rock. And when they, too, are in a land of endless sand and all sorts and varieties of lime-stone and clays.

But those who have made modern Florida—the Florida of the last fifty years—have apparently never thought architecturally except in terms of their own Northern towns. In these strange scenes they wanted something familiar. And as for the coquina and coral rock, why bother with them when there were endless pine forests, and they knew so well what to do with a saw-mill. And so the hotels and homes and shops of Florida towns, with a few interesting exceptions, were painted frame buildings, hastily constructed on Northern models, and very often the builders rooted out the cocoanut pine, the poinsetta and the bougain-villea and brought down nice and proper maples and lilacs and woodbines "just like home."

IT DIDN'T have a thing to do with Florida, and that was what Addison Mizner saw at a glance when he first came to the country early in 1918—a sick man looking for rest, an architect, too, and was asked to build, not a house but a hospital, by his host and friend, Paris Singer. Singer had built a hospital for the French and one for the English, and now he had come back to his own country and he wanted one in the South for convalescing soldiers. He and Mizner talked much of it. It must be Spanish. "The blue skies and pastelle ocean didn't look like a New England farmhouse to me," he says. And he went at it with passion and energy, working through all that hot summer of 1918, in a frenzied effort to have it ready by fall for those who would need it. Then came the end of the War, and Mr. Singer decided he would turn the hospital into a club— The Everglades, they called it.

Now, while Addison Mizner had been building, Palm Beach had been looking on with hostile eyes. He was doing a thing which the natural beauty of the place cried for. But it was so different from what they were used to, they said he was spoiling the town. There was even talk of injunctions. But he went on, making a thing, Spanish in type, but with not a vestige of slavery to any type. "I didn't dare tell them that it was not a really Spanish thing I was doing," he said once. "What I really did was to turn the Spanish inside out like a glove, making all the openings face a patio or court yard. I made every room face two or three ways." What he meant was simply this. Your Spanish house, your Spanish public building was really a fortification—until perhaps fifty years ago—thick walls; narrow barred windows, heavily shuttered—all its charm and lightness within. Its courts and corridors and balconies, its high windows and little galleries, with outside staircases, joyful things but necessarily protected by a severe outside just as the towns, big and little, had to be protected from the brigands and raiders who infested the land. There was no call for fortifications at Palm Beach. The pirates that came there led a legalized existence. They might strip you of your jewels and your pocketbook but it was done in a recognized and protected gambling house. What Mizner sought was to give to the outside as well as the inside, gaiety, lightness and openness, free access of all to the sun and air of the country. He must have this to carry out his desire that everybody who came to Florida should be able, day and night, to fill his lungs with its marvelous air, be always in the sun, if he so desired.

AND SO the club was finished as he would have it, and opened to the public; and he tells you how he sat behind the palms with a heavy heart while the public came to see. With what amazement as well as happiness he heard their surprised and delighted comments; "How beautiful!" "How it belongs!" "What a revelation!"

Now, Palm Beach at that time, the close of the War, was full of the rich. The Riviera was still closed to them, but they were beginning to learn that they had the makings of as beautiful a Riviera as there is on the globe, within easy reach of their Northern homes. Mizner had shown them by his Everglades Club that it was possible to achieve in Florida, a beauty and a charm very like the thing that they felt along the Mediterranean, but which no one had ever known how really to give them along the Florida coast.

CALLS FOR houses flowed upon him. One cannot pick and choose, as I said, though of course you cannot speak of Mizner's work without speaking of what is certainly one of the most perfect great houses in America, the Cosden Villa. I had the same impression in looking on its exterior the first time, that I had had at my first glimpse of The Cloister at Boca Raton, the sense of somebody knowing what he was about and not afraid of the kind of thing he was handling. Spanish—yes. But, like all great architecture, all great buildings, with the feel of growth in it, and with some sense of the future. Addison Mizner's historic sense is strong. It flows through all his work. He apparently is never satisfied in building unless he can give a hint of tradition, of romance, an impression of the centuries it has taken to create the great houses, the great cathedrals of the world. "The transition of art has become my greatest enjoyment," he says. "Most modern architects have spent their lives carrying out a period to the last letter and producing a characterless copybook effect. My ambition has been to take the reverse stand—to make a building look traditional and as though it had fought its way from a small unimportant structure to a great rambling house that took centuries of different needs and ups and downs of wealth to accomplish. I sometimes start a house with a Romanesque corner, pretend that it has fallen into disrepair and been added to in the Gothic spirit, when suddenly the great wealth of the New World has poured in and the owner had added a very rich Renaissance addition." All of this one sees in the Cosden Villa.

He does not miss a trick in getting the full value of the ocean—the very feet of the Cosden house are in the ocean. You sit on its balconies or walk its terraces and you seem to hang over the water. As you enter the front door, you have straight ahead, framed in a severe Gothic arch, a glimpse of the sea. It is managed by a tunnel which runs through the house and under the terrace above the sea wall to the beach. Along this tunnel are the doors into the bathing houses. It is one of the cunning and yet enticing devices in which Mizner delights.

THE COSDEN VILLA is splendid and spacious within—great staircases, great walls, great halls and great rooms. The beauty and interest of the things within are endless, but they do not bother you or overpower you. They all belong, contributing to a livable harmony, and you move about it quite unawed and so entirely satisfied with the loveliness of the thing.

But this club, these houses are not the most likable things that Addison Mizner has given to Palm Beach; those are his street, the Via Mizner; his own house, the Villa Mizner. This little street is open to all the world. You must have your card to go to The Everglades, and your invitation to pass the door of the houses, and only a favored few can negotiate them, but you enter the little street freely and its pink, blue and cream-colored fronts, its gay little shops, its cafés, the chairs on the sidewalks, give you a real sense of what a Florida town might be if it could escape the domination of the Northern town.

Mizner's own house is the biggest and most important thing in the Via Mizner. There are many delightful features in that house and many rarely beautiful things, but nothing quite goes to the heart of the worker like the study—a loggia in the tower which is part of the building. Two floors make up the bulk of the house—the tower has four—the top room, a great square place, windows on all four sides, is a work room with splendid volumes from every country in the world, studies of the world's architecture, endless portfolios of photographs and etchings and drawings—a collection, too, of those fascinating early maps of the Florida coast, the Gulf and the islands to the South.

It is from that room that one sees best a something that Mizner talks much of, and that is the Florida skyline and what it should be—not the forced unnatural imitation of Northern commercial skylines, things endlessly up into the air. There is no call here, along this long Atlantic front, to run up; the natural thing is to run along. "But we want a skyline," they tell you. But look out from Mizner's window and see the true Florida skyline—those red tiled roofs, peaked, variable, at different elevations, and all at such a height that the thing which makes the most beauty against the sky in all Florida, the palm, receives its full value.

WHAT MIZNER had done in Palm Beach was like a revelation to me. You need not ruin the enchantment of Florida by development. You could preserve it all, enhance it even, if you only knew how—and he knew how. And right away I felt that there was a kind of sacred duty before beauty lovers to see that Boca Raton, to which I had been allured by its name and its tradition of pirates, but which, after all, I had thought of only as another development in a country which seemed to be swamped in developments, should not be allowed to die, that is if Addison Mizner could do its building.

BUT WHERE had he learned it all? I, little familiar, to be sure, with the world of architecture, yet flattering myself that I knew most of its great names, I had never heard of Addison Mizner. Where had he learned how to handle a type so surely, so joyfully and to fit it so perfectly to landscape, to climate, to natural resources! Of course I could not leave until I had at least a hint, and it was sitting in the tower room and prodding him—for he has to be prodded to talk about himself, having great humility in his work, being always overwhelmed with the idea that he might have done so much better, whatever he has accomplished, being, too, a humorous being, detesting self-complacency and strutting. But if you keep at it long enough, you will find out things about him.

You will find that he was born in California in 1872—pioneer stock on both sides. For three hundred years or more, the Mizners and the Watsons—

Mrs. Mizner was a Watson—had been steadily venturing on new and uncharted roads. Lansing Mizner, Addison's father, was a soldier in the Mexican War at sixteen, and there became a major, passing the sword at the surrender of Buena Vista and the city of Mexico. In 1848 he was in California, and there for the rest of his life he practiced law.

It was in San Francisco that Lansing Mizner married his wife—a girl who had seen even more of the perils of the pioneer's life than the man she married. One of her first recollections was of shooting Indians from an upper window of a cabin, up near the headwaters of the Mississippi. Another was of floating down the Mississippi in an open boat, with only her mother and little brother and sisters as companions. They were going to St. Louis to search for Mr. Watson, who had left them to establish a home in Missouri. He did not return so they went alone to find him, and they did find him, ill of typhoid.

STILL LATER the little girl remembered weeks of migration westward to California, via the Isthmus of Panama—a journey ending in horrible disaster and the drowning of her only brother, when their ship, the "Independence," was wrecked in March 1853 on the reefs of the bleak and desolate Margareta Island. But few of the four hundred and more passengers escaped, among them Mr. and Mrs. Watson and their three little girls. There was a hideous wait of three days, without food, shelter or water. By chance they were rescued and taken to San Francisco, and it was here that Ella Watson grew up, to become famous not only as the most beautiful woman of her time in California, but to her end in 1915, a typical *grande dame*.

When Addison Mizner talks of "Mamma Mizner" as he calls her, he will tell you of her love and sympathy for youth, of her unacquaintance with the meaning of the word "fear," that she never knew what the back of a chair was made for, that she had the most perfect sense of humor and the most placid soul that he has ever known. No wonder he has dreamed all his life of building her a cathedral.

"MAMMA MIZNER" brought a big family of children into the world —"a ton and a half of them," Addison tells you with pride. He was the sixth boy. "There were so many of us," he declares, "that one learned brevity of speech as the only method of wedging in an idea." And as he was shy and sensitive the prompt challenge from the bevy of older brothers that met every idea he ventured to suggest frequently shut up his mouth for months.

There was his invention of a pie lifter. He had been watching the cook's difficulty in turning the pie around in the oven, and quickly his inventive nature—the authenticity of which he had not yet established, in the minds of his elders in the tribe, though since there is no doubt that they have come to it—went to work. He announced that he had invented a pie lifter—an idea which of course was promptly howled down. "This did not kill my inventive genius," Addison Mizner says, "but it kept it under cover for many years."

BUT if he was not allowed to express himself in inventions, he was obliged to with his fists. You have to fight your way when you have five older brothers, also you have to fight your way in the public school. The boys in the public schools of Bernicia, outside of San Francisco, where the family went early to live, had revolted against soap and water. They would have nothing to do with clean faces and hands and garments; but this was one point on which "Mamma Mizner" would never compromise—her prejudice the other way being quite as strong as that of the youngsters in school, so Addison was obliged to stand up, day by day, against the united attack of the young revolutionists. It was a training—a training which was to be useful later, as we shall see.

It is probable that in these early years he had not yet discovered that the strongest thing in him was his love of beautiful things, and that to make them in his own way would be the only satisfaction his soul could know on earth. Possibly he would have been much longer in finding it out than he was if when he was twelve or thirteen years old he had not splintered his leg—an ugly accident that kept him in bed for months.

WHILE OTHER BOYS were playing games, going to school, getting the education of association with those of their own age and kind, young Addison, propped up in bed, found, probably to his mother's relief as well as to his own delight, that he was getting just as much fun, working with pencils and crayons on drawing paper as ever he had with games outside, and also getting a certain relief from the drills in studies which never in the least had interested him, like mathematics and spelling.

It was while he was still a cripple that his father was sent by the United States Government as a special envoy to Central America, his mission being to settle troubles between Costa Rica and Nicaragua and at the same time to look into the Canal situation, the popular interest at that time being in Nicaragua rather than Panama.

MR. MIZNER took his whole family with him to Guatemala, where they were to live. Addison was put to school at the Instituto Nationale where he learned Spanish, and other things; but what principally filled his thoughts was the ravishing beauty around him. Scattered over Guatemala's plains and up her mountain sides were transplanted bits of the Old World, most of them dating from the sixteenth century, when the first capitol was built. Spain in settling this country had given enormous grants of land to hundreds of her impoverished nobles. Those that migrated to the New World had made immense fortunes and had used their money freely in importing beautiful things for their convents, monasteries and haciendas.

Addison Mizner will tell you that some of the very finest things he has ever collected he has found in Guatemala, things brought from Spain by these early gentlemen of noble traditions and tastes. It was not only the beauty of things about him that aroused him, but it was the romance, the excitement, the adventure in a country where assassination was the favorite method of settling governmental disputes and getting rid of presidents factions did not like.

About the time that the Mizners had gone to Guatemala, Rufino Barrios, president of the State for twelve or more years, a man who had gone far in his attempt to modernize his country, had been assassinated. His nephew, Rapheno Barrios, was an aspirant for the presidency. Addison came to know him, became his romantic supporter, and as chance would have it, was able to save him from an attempted assassination. The story of this adventure he later told to Richard Harding Davis, who, quick to see its romantic and heroic side, made from it his famous "Soldier of Fortune." Addison Mizner, with a few years and a necessary sweetheart added, is the hero of that famous and enthralling tale.

IT WAS in Guatemala, surrounded as he was by the marvelous adaptations of Spanish architecture, that Addison Mizner came to his resolve that he would be an artist, probably an architect. But the family hooted and when they went back to California, as they did after a four years' stay, he was promptly put in school. He tells me, a little ruefully, not boastfully at all, that he was a "rotten bad student, who could not spell in any language." Sixty was his "top." "I try to make myself believe," he says, "that the subjects I was examined in were not the subjects I was interested in, that had they examined me in observation, history, the joy of things beautiful, my delight in color as well as form, I might have gone as high as sixty-five—perhaps not. Looking back, I fear I was both inattentive and mischievous, that I took much more delight in giggling and getting others to giggle than I did in either mathematics or spelling."

His distaste for academic training had something to do, no doubt, with the consent of his family that he should enter a Spanish and not an American university; and so, at eighteen, he went abroad, to Salamanca in Spain. And here again, it was beauty — the beauty of buildings, of towns, of all sorts of things that men had made with their hands which fascinated him; his sketch book probably received much more attention than the sciences or philosophies. It was here, surrounded as he was by the accumulation of centuries of beautiful creation, that the collector Mizner seems to have been born. "Thou shalt not covet," he says, "was the command that I broke most often and generally I broke it hardest in the great churches and monasteries. Not always being able to afford the things myself, I, little by little, started to collect, selling the things that I least coveted, which gave me money enough to hold onto the dearest possessions.

"It would be a hard thing for me to pick out even a short list of the really fine things that I have brought to America, for I have looted cathedrals, churches and palaces, and brought a shipload or two of everything from stone doorways to fine laces from both Central America and Europe. It was early that I recognized that the top note of art in each century was the Madonna and the crucifix, so I began collecting these for myself."

ALL OF THIS saturation with beauty, this possession of and association with beautiful pieces, unfitted him more and more for schools. He determined that he had done with them, that he was going to see the world. And he started out on his own to do it.

In the next few years Addison Mizner found his way even into the islands of the Pacific. He had to make his way or beat it, and his equipment for bread-earning was small. However, the two things in which he seemed to have taken a genuine interest up to this time—boxing before his accident, drawing after it—both served to get him out of more than one tight place.

He was in Honolulu, his money gone, when he fell in with a photographer who was making enlargements of fat Hawaiian ladies and serious looking Chinese merchants. He joined him and the two set up a business in charcoal drawings—"horrible charcoal drawings," Mizner describes them as being, "with red velvet mats and frames that matched." In a few months the two made $3,000 apiece, on what he calls "this low deceit." With that money in his pocket, he moved on to see new countries and new beauties.

THE NEXT time his pockets were empty, he refilled them by coloring lantern slides for a traveling lecturer. This enterprise took him to Australia, where the traveling lecturer gave up his venture, and Mizner found himself so low in funds that he was obliged to eat at a lunch counter where the chief guests were prize fighters. He soon became more or less friendly with the gentry, even boxing a little with them. His reputation as an amateur became so respectable that on the failure of one of the champions to turn up at an advertised prize fight, for which a large audience had gathered, Mizner accepted an invitation to take his place, his opponent promising him that he would not knock him out until the fourth round. But Mizner was still on his feet in the tenth, though he confesses that, by this round, he was spending most of the time in keeping out of the way.

The next week he issued a challenge to the champion for a return bout, provided they would give him a third of the gate receipts. He concedes that the boxer must have been pretty bad, for in the fourth round he laid him out flat. The gate receipts were enough to enable him to return again to a class of society, which, if possibly less interesting, was really more to his taste.

ALL OF these wanderings about may have seemed futile enough to orderly minded people, but Mizner himself knew—possibly not very clearly, but still knew—what he was after. All of these experiences only intensified his youthful determination to be an artist—an architect. He decided to settle down now, settle down in Europe and study its masterpieces.

Young men determined to be architects, who can go to Europe, generally seek the Beaux Arts, but he did not want the Beaux Arts. He wanted to learn architecture by studying architecture—architecture of all kinds. So now, sketch book in hand, he spent many months going about Europe getting acquainted with its public buildings, its great palaces, particularly its great cathedrals. After soaking himself to his heart's content in all this and having accumulated an immense stock of sketches, photographs, engravings—tools for his trade—he determined it was time to get to work. So back to California he went—to San Francisco.

THERE WAS an architect there that could understand his unorthodox education. That was Willis Polk. He was radical enough to understand Addison Mizner when he said he could not see why in the world the Temple of Diana of Ephesus should be reproduced in Norway or by the side of the Panama Canal.

But they evidently had no chance to reproduce even temples of Diana. What the Californians in their vicinity asked of them was the building of bungalows, the mending of sinks. And that was what Addison Mizner was busy about when there suddenly turned up in San Francisco his Guatemalian friend, Rapheno Barrios, now president and dictator of that turbulent State.

SENORA BARRIOS, an American woman, was with him. And they looked up Mizner. Would he, they asked, accept a commission to build and furnish a new palace in Guatemala. The commission they offered was immense. There was no hesitation on Addison Mizner's part. He threw his bungalows and his sinks to the winds, cashed in on his entire possessions and started out to celebrate his good fortune. About the time he had spent everything he had, a steamer arrived from the State of Guatemala, bringing, instead of the retainer fee he expected, the news that the young dictator, Barrios, had been assassinated.

One could hardly expect even a well regulated scion of the Beaux Arts to go back to bungalows and sinks after such a dream. Nothing now would cure him of the blow but new adventure, and still more adventure. It was at hand. One of his older brothers, who was at the head of the Alaska Commercial Company, was preparing at that moment to set out on an expedition into the then unknown Yukon country, where they proposed to establish trading posts. It was a good business. "A sack of flour would bring twenty silver-tipped fox skins and a tin of tomatoes as many as thirty ermine pelts," says Addison. So he joined his brother and soon was exploring the head waters of the Yukon and the adjacent lakes and country. With their equipment packed on their backs the little party trekked over precipitous mountains, shot rapids, dropped over waterfalls, going on and on into an uncharted and unexplored region—strenuous business for a young man reared as he had been and handicapped by a crippled leg. For four months they traveled in this land without seeing a human being, then one day, suddenly, as they floated down the Yukon, they came upon five persons.

THEY IMMEDIATELY put to shore and heard the story of how a little while before Jack McQuestion and his wife, when scraping out their frying pan with sand had found there was gold in a little stream called the Trondick, later to be called the Klondike. The Mizner party tarried to build McQuestion a cabin. Before the cabin was completed the country began to fill up with prospectors and traders, for the discovery of gold has a mysterious way of penetrating from the most remote places to the outside world and of drawing people, no matter what the hardships of approach.

Obviously this was the place for the first of the new trading posts that the elder Mizner had set out to establish. There was need of an architect and Addison's first order was for a two-story log cabin 22 ft. wide by 60 ft. long— the architectural triumph of the Northland, a building worthy of its cost, which was something like $120,000.00.

He spent two years along the Yukon. There was little chance for further architectural triumphs though there were plenty of log cabins for him to build, and there was a tremendous chance for hardening of muscle and of will, and of learning better than he had ever had a chance before of what makes weaklings, of what a better class really means, those that stand the gaff. He will tell you that whatever there was of the snob in him died in Alaska. He learned there what is real in life as well as in people. But after all, Alaska was no more than another adventure. He must go back to his own, the study and the making of beauty—find a place where he could create—and after a dip into the Orient, perhaps to take the taste of too much Alaska out of his mouth, he settled in New York.

HE FOUND in New York the value of authority, of being a regular Beaux Arts man. He didn't belong. But people found that he could make beautiful things—the Spanish kind of thing. His orders grew. He went back to Guatemala, his boyish love, remembering its treasures well enough to know where to put his hands on rare, lovely objects for his New York customers.

But he over-worked. The War brought him worries. His shattered leg was troublesome. Ill and possibly a little discouraged, he went to Palm Beach as I have told, the guest of Paris Singer. And then it became clear to others as well as to himself just what all that architectural education of his had prepared him for. He evidently was born to create in Florida a type of architecture suitable to her climate and her palms, to adapt the Spanish so that it fitted.

HOW WELL prepared he was to do what was needed that first summer of 1918 showed. One who built in Florida at that time ought to understand what it meant for Pharoah to require the Jews to make bricks without straw. The country was practically without workers. It was impossible to get any kind of supplies. The solidity of Addison Mizner's preparation came out brilliantly in this crisis.

In all of his wanderings over the world, studying buildings, looking, sketching, he had never been content until he knew how the thing that attracted him was made. He must know just how stones were laid. How was it that they could be laid without cement or clutches so perfectly that they would stand centuries of wear, like the Etruscan walls of Siena? How were some of these cements made that had lasted through the centuries?

WHAT WERE these woods? How were they seasoned, combined? And where did those marbles come from? How were they transported, worked? How did the Spaniards get these irregular shapes for their roof tiles? The color of these glazes? That rough surface in the plaster? None of the things that had awakened his sense of beauty ever went unchallenged. He studied with his hands as well as with his eyes, not satisfied until he could do the thing. The result was that when he went to Florida he was, as he says himself, "as good a bricklayer as any man I ever had. I can plaster as well as any plasterer I have ever seen. I am a fairly good carpenter, a better than ordinary electrician. I know how to wipe a joint in plumbing. One has to know these things, otherwise you cannot get done the thing that you want done, for there is the eternal objection, 'it can't be done that way.' I know enough to say, 'we will do it that way, I know how to do it.'"

It was this knowledge of the rudiments of his profession that made it possible, when he attacked the problem of building at Palm Beach, to make the things that he wanted and to train others—untrained Negroes principally, there being little other labor left in the country. He wanted fireplaces for the chilly nights that do happily come occasionally even in Florida's summer—but there were no bricklayers in the town—nobody built chimneys in Palm Beach, possibly to prove that it is never frosty there, so Mizner had to take green labor and teach it bricklaying.

He wanted tiles for his roofs—irregular tiles. It was not possible to bring them from the countries where they are made, for there was still an embargo on shipments. He knew how in Spain they were moulded over a man's thigh, so he made moulds over his own and other men's thighs, a sufficient variety, setting up his own terra cotta factory in West Palm Beach, and himself producing what he could not buy and what he felt he must have in order to secure that first beauty, so essential to the thing he was after, the irregular tiled roof. There was difficulty about clays for the terra cotta. Florida clays have been little developed, but in Georgia there was what he needed, so immediately he began to import it. As the demand for more houses and more houses grew, the factory, which at the start was no more than a small shed with a baking kiln, spread until there were several acres of sheds and kilns and storage rooms.

BUT IT WAS not only roof tiles that he must have. He wanted floor tiles, wall tiles, urns, pots, fountains, all the brightly colored things that one finds along the Mediterranean. Almost before those looking on realized it, Mizner had established a great industry, turning out a wealth of glazed articles. The coloring of these was particularly successful, for colors he knew, and how to mix them. That was another thing he had learned in his years of wandering. Some of the shades that were developed were so unusual that they took his name. There is a Mizner blue that every builder has come to know.

But there were other things that Mizner wanted. There was antique furniture. It was easy enough to procure it but often it did not stand the Palm Beach climate with its extreme damp in the summer rainy season. Iron nails rusted, leather mildewed and any veneered woodwork came unglued and fell to pieces during the first summer. So Mizner started a wood-carving and furniture constructing factory to make durable and usable copies of antiques to fit the local needs. He imported enormous quantities of the finest grade of Italian walnut logs. None of the products were glued or veneered in the usual trade manner, but carefully joined and pegged and made to last indefinitely. An iron forge was also added for the construction of lamps, candlesticks, railings, balconies, grills, door latches, hinges and the thousand and one other accessories that were needed. These hand wrought iron articles adapted from Spanish patterns are almost limitless in number and variety.

A CASTING WORKS was also added. This was necessary because Florida has very little native stone. All forms of imitation lime, stone, granite, even marbles in color were produced and the finest grade of casting resulted. Mr. Mizner originated a special process by which doorways, window frames and fountains, which were cast were afterward machine tooled all over, which more nearly imitated the effect of hand cut stone than any other means that could be found. He also developed unusual ways of adding some of the charm of age to stonework by means of the sand blasting machine and various sorts of stains and colorings.

He introduced as well a department to make stained and leaded glass windows.

THERE WERE many discouragements in the early days of the "Las Manos" ("handmade") factory. Several times the chimneys of the brick kilns collapsed and smashed hundreds of tiles in the baking. Once during the second year, the entire shed burned down and all the equipment was lost. It was soon reconstructed however, and expanded larger than ever. There was, too, the eternal difficulty of finding skilled workmen in the various crafts for the more skilled work and keeping them on the spot, in addition to the trials of training ignorant and unskilled Negroes for the rougher work.

There you have the man—the man that won't be stopped in getting what he wants for his work. No tiles? Mould them over your thigh, build a kiln, bake them yourself. No bricklayer? Teach a Negro. Your furniture falls apart? Go across the sea for the wood you want and peg the parts together. No blue that suits the scene? Mix one—and so it goes, and if there is no one to build a chimney properly or plaster to suit one's need or mend the pipe, do it yourself. To know these things and to be able to show others how to do them is as much a part of your profession as planning, designing, adapting.

ONLY a man mad for beauty and one who was too a pioneer and an adventurer could have worked his way to the place Addison Mizner has taken in Florida. He is what he is by inheritance as well as by giving free reign to that inheritance. His love of beauty comes down through his mother from Sir Joshua Reynolds himself—his great grand-uncle. As for pioneering and adventuring, Watsons and Mizners for generations before him have rarely let a chance for either, or both preferably, escape.

His work in Florida is a pioneer work—"our last frontier" the Floridians call their land—and it is an adventure—a rare one—an adventure in creating the particular lovely things that will give full value to the charms of a lovely land.

ILLUSTRATIONS

RESIDENCE *of* ADDISON MIZNER
Entrance from Via Mizner

RESIDENCE *of* ADDISON MIZNER
Entrance Hall

[2]

RESIDENCE *of* ADDISON MIZNER
Doorway of living room

RESIDENCE of ADDISON MIZNER

Living room

RESIDENCE of ADDISON MIZNER

Living room

RESIDENCE OF ADDISON MIZNER

Dining room

R ESIDENCE *of* A DDISON M IZNER
Tower room

RESIDENCE *of* ADDISON MIZNER

View from tower room

RESIDENCE *of* ADDISON MIZNER
Entrance to Via Mizner

VIA MIZNER

Alley of shops

VIA MIZNER

Patio of restaurant

VIA MIZNER

Bridge over shops

VIA PARIGI

Alley of shops

Via Parigi

Yard of Mizner products shop

WORTH AVENUE

Arcade of shops

Everglades Club

EVERGLADES CLUB

Main entrance before additions were built

EVERGLADES CLUB

Cloister entrance

EVERGLADES CLUB
Cloister garden

EVERGLADES CLUB
Vista through court of oranges

EVERGLADES CLUB
The court of oranges

Everglades Club
Court of oranges tea garden

EVERGLADES CLUB
Fountain in the patio

EVERGLADES CLUB

The patio from upper terrace

EVERGLADES CLUB
Ball room

EVERGLADES CLUB

Dining room. Frescoes by Achille Angeli

EVERGLADES CLUB

Hall

EVERGLADES CLUB

Spiral stairs

APARTMENT *of* PARIS SINGER *in* EVERGLADES CLUB

Living room

APARTMENT of PARIS SINGER in EVERGLADES CLUB

APARTMENT of PARIS SINGER in EVERGLADES CLUB
Living room windows

APARTMENT *of* PARIS SINGER *in* EVERGLADES CLUB

SINGER BUILDING *on* ROYAL PALM WAY

THE PLAZA SHOPS *on* PALM BEACH AVENUE

THE PLAZA SHOPS *on* PALM BEACH AVENUE
Patio

GULF STREAM GOLF CLUB

GULF STREAM GOLF CLUB
Main entrance stairs

GULF STREAM GOLF CLUB

The terrace

GULF STREAM GOLF CLUB

Dining room

THE CLOISTER at BOCA RATON
Florida

THE CLOISTER *at* BOCA RATON

Main entrance

THE CLOISTER *at* BOCA RATON

Main entrance door

THE CLOISTER *at* BOCA RATON
Main entrance hall

THE CLOISTER *at* BOCA RATON
Dining room

THE CLOISTER *at* BOCA RATON
Doorway from ball room to loggia

THE CLOISTER *at* BOCA RATON

THE CLOISTER *at* BOCA RATON
Fireplace in ball room

THE CLOISTER *at* BOCA RATON

THE CLOISTER *at* BOCA RATON
The terrace

THE CLOISTER *at* BOCA RATON

The loggia

THE CLOISTER *at* BOCA RATON

The patio

THE CLOISTER *at* BOCA RATON
Vista of cloisters

The Cloister *at* Boca Raton
Cloisters

THE CLOISTER *at* BOCA RATON

THE CLOISTER *at* BOCA RATON

View of garage from tower

ADMINISTRATION BUILDING *at* BOCA RATON
Main entrance doorway

Administration Building *at* Boca Raton

Large patio

ADMINISTRATION BUILDING *at* BOCA RATON

Small patio

RIVERSIDE BAPTIST CHURCH, JACKSONVILLE

Facade

RIVERSIDE BAPTIST CHURCH, JACKSONVILLE

RIVERSIDE BAPTIST CHURCH, JACKSONVILLE
Baptistry

"El Sarimento", Residence *of* A. J. Drexel Biddle, Jr.

Entrance doorway

"El Sarimento", Residence of A. J. Drexel Biddle, Jr.
The patio

"El Sarimento", Residence of A. J. Drexel Biddle, Jr.

RESIDENCE OF ARTHUR B. CLAFLIN

View from Lake Worth

RESIDENCE of ARTHUR B. CLAFLIN

The water gate

RESIDENCE OF ARTHUR B. CLAFLIN
Terrace on Lake Worth

RESIDENCE *of* ARTHUR B. CLAFLIN

The terrace

RESIDENCE *of* ARTHUR B. CLAFLIN
The patio

RESIDENCE of ARTHUR B. CLAFLIN
Entrance from patio

RESIDENCE of ARTHUR B. CLAFLIN

Hall and stairs

Residence *of* Arthur B. Claflin

"Playa Riente", Residence *of* Mrs. Hugh Dillman (formerly of Joshua S. Cosden)

Ocean front

[73]

"PLAYA RIENTE", RESIDENCE *of* MRS. HUGH DILLMAN (FORMERLY OF JOSHUA S. COSDEN)

Stairway to beach

"PLAYA RIENTE", RESIDENCE *of* MRS. HUGH DILLMAN (FORMERLY OF JOSHUA S. COSDEN)

View from garden

"Playa Riente", Residence of Mrs. Hugh Dillman (formerly of Joshua S. Cosden)

"PLAYA RIENTE", RESIDENCE *of* MRS. HUGH DILLMAN (FORMERLY OF JOSHUA S. COSDEN)

Main entrance doorway

"Playa Riente", Residence *of* Mrs. Hugh Dillman (formerly of Joshua S. Cosden)

Vista of ocean through tunnel

"PLAYA RIENTE", RESIDENCE *of* MRS. HUGH DILLMAN (FORMERLY OF JOSHUA S. COSDEN)
Main entrance hall and north stairway

"PLAYA RIENTE", RESIDENCE *of* MRS. HUGH DILLMAN (FORMERLY OF JOSHUA S. COSDEN)

Main entrance hall and south stairway

"Playa Riente", Residence of Mrs. Hugh Dillman (formerly of Joshua S. Cosden)

Hall outside of dining room

"Playa Riente", Residence of Mrs. Hugh Dillman (formerly of Joshua S. Cosden)
Italian dining room *Frescoes by Achille Angeli*

"Playa Riente", Residence of Mrs. Hugh Dillman (formerly of Joshua S. Cosden)

Italian dining room   Frescoes by *Achille Angeli*

"Playa Riente", Residence of Mrs. Hugh Dillman (formerly of Joshua S. Cosden)

Spanish bar-room

"PLAYA RIENTE", RESIDENCE *of* MRS. HUGH DILLMAN (FORMERLY OF JOSHUA S. COSDEN)

The Spanish bar

[85]

"PLAYA RIENTE", RESIDENCE *of* MRS. HUGH DILLMAN (FORMERLY *of* JOSHUA S. COSDEN)

"Playa Riente", Residence of Mrs. Hugh Dillman (formerly of Joshua S. Cosden)
Roof terraces

"Casa De Leoni", Residence *of* Robert Glendinning (formerly of leonard thomas)
View from Lake Worth

"Casa De Leoni", Residence of Robert Glendinning (formerly of Leonard Thomas)
Terrace

"Casa De Leoni", Residence *of* Robert Glendinning (formerly of Leonard Thomas)
Venetian doorway

RESIDENCE *of* JOHN F. HARRIS

View of tower

RESIDENCE *of* JOHN F. HARRIS
Main entrance doorway

RESIDENCE OF JOHN F. HARRIS

Patio

RESIDENCE *of* HARRY HASKINS (FORMERLY OF HON. C. T. WYNN)

"La Bellucia", Residence of Dr. Willey Lyon Kingsley

Facade

"La Bellucia", Residence of Dr. Willey Lyon Kingsley

"LA BELLUCIA", RESIDENCE *of* DR. WILLEY LYON KINGSLEY
Fountain in patio

"The Towers", Residence of Stephen A. Lynch (formerly of William M. Wood)

[99]

RESIDENCE of H. P. McGINLEY (FORMERLY OF DANIEL H. CARSTAIRS)

RESIDENCE *of* H. P. McGINLEY (FORMERLY OF DANIEL H. CARSTAIRS)
Entrance from patio

RESIDENCE of H. P. McGINLEY (FORMERLY OF DANIEL H. CARSTAIRS)

RESIDENCE *of* GEORGE LUKE MESKER

Main entrance doorway

RESIDENCE of GEORGE LUKE MESKER

RESIDENCE *of* GEORGE LUKE MESKER
Living room

RESIDENCE of WILSON MIZNER

"Sin Cuidado", Residence of Edward S. Moore

View from ocean boulevard

"Sin Cuidado", Residence of Edward S. Moore
Entrance from patio

"Sin Cuidado", Residence of Edward S. Moore
Gate to patio

"Sin Cuidado", Residence of Edward S. Moore

Terraces in patio garden

"SIN CUIDADO", RESIDENCE of EDWARD S. MOORE
Stairs

"Sin Cuidado", Residence of Edward S. Moore

Living room

"Sin Cuidado", Residence of Edward S. Moore

Dining room

[113]

"Collado Hueco", Residence of Paul Moore

Main entrance

"Collado Hueco", Residence *of* Paul Moore

The patio

[115]

"COLLADO HUECO", RESIDENCE OF PAUL MOORE

Living room

"COLLADO HUECO", RESIDENCE OF PAUL MOORE

Dining room

"Louwana", Residence of Gurnee Munn

Facade

"LOUWANA", RESIDENCE of GURNEE MUNN

Patio

"Amado", Residence of Charles Munn

"AMADO", RESIDENCE of CHARLES MUNN
Main entrance hall

"Casa Bendita", Residence of John S. Phipps

"Casa Bendita", Residence *of* John S. Phipps

Patio, stairway and tower

"Casa Bendita", Residence *of* John S. Phipps

The loggia

"CASA BENDITA", RESIDENCE *of* JOHN S. PHIPPS

Swimming pool

RESIDENCE of GEORGE S. RASMUSSEN

[126]

RESIDENCE of GEORGE S. RASMUSSEN

Patio

"Lagomar", Residence of Henry Rea (formerly of John Magee)

"Lagomar", Residence *of* Henry Rea (formerly of john magee)

Entrance driveway

[129]

"LAGOMAR", RESIDENCE *of* HENRY REA (FORMERLY OF JOHN MAGEE)

The patio

"Lagomar", Residence of Henry Rea (formerly of John Magee)

The patio

"Lagomar", Residence of Henry Rea (formerly of John Magee)

"VILLA TRANQUILLA", RESIDENCE OF DE GRIMM RENFRO

Side entrance

"VILLA TRANQUILLA", RESIDENCE *of* DE GRIMM RENFRO
The patio

"Casa Florencia", Residence of Dr. Preston Pope Satterwhite

Facade

"Casa Florencia", Residence of Dr. Preston Pope Satterwhite

View from the Mirador

"Casa Florencia", Residence *of* Dr. Preston Pope Satterwhite
The patio

"Casa Florencia", Residence of Dr. Preston Pope Satterwhite

"Casa Florencia", Residence *of* Dr. Preston Pope Satterwhite
Vista of patio

"Casa Florencia", Residence *of* Dr. Preston Pope Satterwhite

Vista of loggia

"Casa Florencia", Residence of Dr. Preston Pope Satterwhite
Main stairway

"Casa Florencia", Residence *of* Dr. Preston Pope Satterwhite

The Gothic dining room

"Casa Florencia", Residence *of* Dr. Preston Pope Satterwhite

The Gothic dining room

"Casa Florencia", Residence of Dr. Preston Pope Satterwhite

Living room

"Villa Flora", Residence of Edward Shearson

Facade

"Villa Flora", Residence of Edward Shearson

"Villa Flora", Residence *of* Edward Shearson

Stairs and cloister

"Concha Marina", Residence *of* George Sloan

Entrance to patio

"Concha Marina", Residence of George Sloan

The patio

RESIDENCE *of* JOSEPH SPEIDEL

Side entrance

RESIDENCE *of* JOSEPH SPEIDEL

The patio

"El Mirasol", Residence *of* Edward T. Stotesbury

Entrance gateway

"El Mirasol", Residence of Edward T. Stotesbury

View from ocean boulevard

[153]

"El Mirasol", Residence of Edward T. Stotesbury

Vista from garden

"El Mirasol", Residence *of* Edward T. Stotesbury
South loggia

"EL MIRASOL", RESIDENCE of EDWARD T. STOTESBURY

The patio

"El Mirasol", Residence of Edward T. Stotesbury

Patio fountain

"El Mirasol", Residence of Edward T. Stotesbury

"El Mirasol", Residence of Edward T. Stotesbury

Entrance hall

"El Mirasol", Residence *of* Edward T. Stotesbury
Moorish cloister

"El Mirasol", Residence of Edward T. Stotesbury

Living room

"El Mirasol", Residence *of* Edward T. Stotesbury

Main stairway

"El Mirasol", Residence *of* Edward T. Stotesbury
Entrance to Moorish tea house

"El Mirasol", Residence of Edward T. Stotesbury

Patio of Moorish tea house

"El Salano", Residence of Harold Vanderbilt

Facade

"El Salano", Residence of Harold Vanderbilt

"El Salano", Residence of Harold Vanderbilt

Living room

"El Salano", Residence of Harold Vanderbilt

Dining room

"La Guerida", Residence of Rodman Wanamaker

Facade

"La Guerida", Residence *of* Rodman Wanamaker
Patio

"Casa Maria Marrone", Residence of Barclay Warburton

East view from Lake Worth

"Casa Maria Marrone", Residence of Barclay Warburton

"Casa Maria Marrone", Residence *of* Barclay Warburton

Vista toward Lake Worth

"Casa Maria Marrone", Residence of Barclay Warburton

RESIDENCE *of* WILLIAM GRAY WARDEN
Main entrance doorway

RESIDENCE *of* WILLIAM GRAY WARDEN

Facade

RESIDENCE *of* WILLIAM GRAY WARDEN
The patio

[177]

RESIDENCE *of* WILLIAM GRAY WARDEN
Fountain in patio

Residence *of* William Gray Warden
Spiral stairway tower

RESIDENCE *of* WILLIAM GRAY WARDEN

View of patio from cloister

RESIDENCE *of* WILLIAM GRAY WARDEN
Vista through cloister

RESIDENCE of WILLIAM GRAY WARDEN
Vista through entrance hall

RESIDENCE *of* WILLIAM GRAY WARDEN
Main stairway

RESIDENCE OF WILLIAM GRAY WARDEN

Living room